pilgrim

CHURCH & KINGDOM
A COURSE FOR THE CHRISTIAN JOURNEY

Church Publishing
NEW YORK

Authors and Contributors

Authors

Stephen Cottrell is the Bishop of Chelmsford
Steven Croft is the Bishop of Sheffield
Paula Gooder is a leading New Testament writer and lecturer
Robert Atwell is the Bishop of Exeter
Sharon Ely Pearson is a Christian educator in The Episcopal Church

Contributors

John Preston is the Church of England's National Stewardship Officer
Rachel Treweek is the Archdeacon of Hackney
Ann Morisy is a community worker and theologian
David Walker is the Bishop of Manchester

pilgrim

CHURCH & KINGDOM
A COURSE FOR THE CHRISTIAN JOURNEY

STEPHEN COTTRELL
STEVEN CROFT
PAULA GOODER
ROBERT ATWELL
SHARON ELY PEARSON

Contributions from
JOHN PRESTON   RACHEL TREWEEK
ANN MORISY   DAVID WALKER

Church Publishing
NEW YORK

Copyright © 2014, 2016 Stephen Cottrell, Steven Croft, Robert Atwell
and Paula Gooder

Cover image—Gajus/Shutterstock.com

ISBN-13: 978-0-89869-952-4 (pbk.)
ISBN-13: 978-0-89869-953-1 (ebook)

First published in the United Kingdom in 2014 by

Church House Publishing
Church House
Great Smith Street
London SW1P 3AZ

First published in the United States in 2016 by

Church Publishing, Incorporated.
19 East 34th Street
New York, New York 10016
www.churchpublishing.org

Cover and contents design by David McNeill, Revo Design.

Library of Congress Cataloging-in-Publication data

A record of this book is available from the Library of Congress.

Printed in the United States of America

CONTENTS

WELCOME TO *PILGRIM*

Welcome to this course of exploration into the truth of the Christian faith as it has been revealed in Jesus Christ and lived out in the Church down through the centuries.

The aim of this course is to help people explore what it means to be disciples of Jesus Christ. From the very beginning of his ministry, Jesus called people to follow him and become his disciples. The first disciples were called to be with Jesus and to be sent out (Mark 3:14). The Church in every generation shares in the task of helping others hear Christ's call to follow him and to live in his service.

The *Pilgrim* material consists of two groups of four short courses. The **Follow** stage is designed for those who are beginning to explore the faith and what following Jesus will mean. It focuses on four great texts that have been particularly significant to Christian people from the earliest days of the Church:

- The Baptismal Covenant (drawn from the Creeds)
- The Lord's Prayer
- The Beatitudes
- The Commandments

The Follow stage is a beginning in the Christian journey. There is much still to be learned. The four courses in the **Grow** stage—of which this is one—aim to take you further and deeper, building on the Follow stage. They focus on:

- The Creeds
- The Eucharist (and the whole life of prayer and worship)

- The Bible
- The Church and the kingdom (living your whole life as a disciple)

We hope that, in the Grow stage, people will learn the essentials for a life of discipleship. We hope that you will do this in the company of a small group of fellow travelers: people like you who want to find out more about the Christian faith and are considering its claims and challenges.

The material in the Grow stage can also be helpful to people who have been Christians for many years, as a way of deepening their discipleship.

We have designed the material in the Grow stage so that it can be led by the members of the group: you don't need an expert or a teacher to guide you through. *Pilgrim* aims to help you learn by encouraging you to practice the ancient disciplines of biblical reflection and prayer which have always been at the heart of the living out of Christian faith.

The format is similar to the Follow stage. Each book has six sessions and, in each session, you will find:

- a **theme**
- some **opening prayers**
- a **"conversation-starter"**
- an opportunity to reflect on a **reading** from Scripture (the Bible)
- a short **reflection** on the theme from a contemporary Christian writer
- some **questions** to address together
- a **"journeying on"** section
- some **closing prayers**
- finally, there are selected quotations from the great tradition of Christian writing to aid further reflection.

You will find a greater emphasis in the Grow stage on learning to tell the story of God's work in your life to others as every disciple is called to be a witness. You will also find a greater emphasis on learning to live out your faith in everyday life. The Journeying On section includes an individual challenge for the week ahead, and you are encouraged to share your progress as part of the Conversation as you meet for the next session.

INTRODUCTION TO
CHURCH & KINGDOM

The New Testament has several different names to describe those who follow Jesus. The first is "followers of the way." This seems quite a good title for people doing a *Pilgrim* course. It speaks of a journey. It suggests that amid the confusions and temptations of the world there is a way to travel through life that makes sense and that will ultimately bring peace and joy. It is the way that is revealed in Jesus, the author and pioneer of our faith (Hebrews 12:2). It says that the Christian faith is first and foremost a way of life rather than a set of things to believe in. Or perhaps a better way of putting it is that there are things to believe in, the things we have explored throughout *Pilgrim*, but they only really make sense when they are lived out.

This module is called *Church & Kingdom*. The title could be misleading. But "following in the way" gives us the clue. We are not chiefly concerned with defining what the Church is beyond the most basic understanding that it is *the people who have been formed by what God has done in Jesus Christ* and are now gathered around him and following his way. And because the kingdom is the governing idea behind so much of Jesus' teaching, namely that in Jesus God's rule of justice and peace is come among us, then to follow in his way means living under God's rule and praying constantly—which of course also means working constantly—for God's kingdom to come on earth.

So that's what this course is about: What does it mean to live as a child of the kingdom of God and follow in the way of Christ each day as a member of the Church? How does it affect our life at work as well as at home? How does it affect what we do with the gifts we have been given, especially those gifts of time and talents, passions, resources, and money? How does it affect our relationships with others? And how does it affect our relationship with the world? How is the Christian faith changing us and shaping us so that we become more like Jesus?

Jesus himself called his followers "disciples," though it is interesting to note that the twelve who were given a preeminent place in his ministry are also called "apostles." Both these names are instructive. A disciple is one who *follows* Jesus and learns from Jesus. An apostle is one who is *sent out*.

In the New Testament there never seems to be a point where the twelve "graduate" from disciple to apostle. They are always both. It must be the same for us. We are the ones who are gathered around Jesus. We are also the ones who are sent out by him. This is the pattern of the Christian life. We keep coming back to Jesus in our prayer and worship and study of the Scriptures; and we need a discipline about this so that our spiritual life is shaped and nourished. This discipline is sometimes called a rule of life. As part of this course we will consider whether such a rule, however basic, should be part of our ongoing discipleship. But at the same time we are sent out by Jesus, commissioned to be his presence in the world, living and serving his purposes in our daily lives. This course will also challenge us to see how we live out our faith on a Monday morning just as much as a Sunday morning.

But of all the names that have been given to describe followers of Jesus, the one that has really stuck is "Christian." This is because to follow Jesus means to be *like Jesus*. How else will people see Jesus today except in and through us? When we say we are witnesses to Christ in our daily lives, we don't just mean that we tell people *about* Jesus, we also mean that everything that Jesus is, and his priorities for the world, and his way of justice, love, and peace, should be *evident in our lives*. Of course, we fall short of such an ideal. This is why examination of life and the sober confession of sin are a vital part of everyday discipleship and every rule of life. But it does not mean the ideal is not worth following.

It is helpful to remember that the followers of Jesus were first called "Christians" in Antioch (see Acts 11:19-26). It was in this cosmopolitan city that the Christian faith broke out from its Jewish roots and started to become a worldwide faith; and it was those who were not part of the faith who called them "Christian" to distinguish them from Jews, but also as a sign that their lives and teaching not only spoke of Christ, but revealed him.

This, I suppose, is one of the big themes of the New Testament: that those who follow Jesus continue his ministry and are his presence in the world. In a climactic passage, rooted in his own conversion experience, the Apostle Paul, who discovered that in persecuting the Church he had persecuted Jesus, calls the Church the "body of Christ," and describes the membership of the Church as being like "limbs and organs" in a body, each with a part to play and each living in harmony and interdependency with the rest (see 1 Corinthians 12:12-27).

Paul also calls followers of Jesus "saints." His letters often begin with a sentence reminding Christians that they are "called to be saints" (see Romans 1:7 and 1 Corinthians 1:2). The word saint means "holy," and although hard to define, holiness is something most of us recognize when we see it. There are some lives that exude a compelling and dynamic closeness to Christ, so that in seeing that person and being with them, it is as if Christ himself were present. This is the greatest gift of the Spirit, which is, of course, the Spirit of Jesus. It is what the Beatitudes describe when they promise that to live this way means to have received—that is, to be actually and already dwelling in—God's kingdom. It is a quality of life and an unspeakable joy that is available to all of us. It doesn't come from hard work, though it does require a daily discipline. It is a gift—the gift of Christ himself that comes when we follow in his way as members of the Church and citizens of God's kingdom. As we live this way we are shaped more and more into Jesus' likeness. We won't really notice it in ourselves, and that is a good thing. If we did, an all too predictable vanity would very quickly regain the ground in our heart and the whole glory of a self-forgetful love would be undone. But others, noting how our lives are rooted in Christ and lived out for his purposes and to his praise and glory, may see Christ in us and follow in his way.

One of the best descriptions of this new life we live in Christ is the Magnificat, the song of praise that Mary sang when she visited her cousin Elizabeth. Like an overflowing fountain, it is a song that breaks forth from the deep wells of Mary's faithfulness to God: she is the one who believes that the Lord's promises will be fulfilled in her (see Luke 1:45). But as well as a song of praise, the Magnificat is also a song of justice: the lowly will be lifted up; the hungry fed.

In this *Pilgrim* course the prayers at the beginning of each session will begin with the Magnificat. It is worth learning it by heart if you can. Throughout the centuries the Church has sung this song of joyful praise and steadfast defiance each evening as part of its set prayer. As we make it our own, so we, like Mary, who is sometimes referred to as the Queen of the Apostles and the first Christian, declare the gathered in and sent out rhythm of prayer and praise, service and action that is our vocation.

Day by day, our lives are changed. We become more like Christ. And the world is changed into the kingdom of God.

STEPHEN COTTRELL

The Magnificat (The Song of Mary)

My soul proclaims the greatness of the Lord,
   my spirit rejoices in God my Savior;
he has looked with favor on his lowly servant.

From this day all generations will call me blessed;
the Almighty has done great things for me
   and holy is his name.

He has mercy on those who fear him,
from generation to generation.

He has shown strength with his arm
and has scattered the proud in their conceit,

Casting down the mighty from their thrones
and lifting up the lowly.

He has filled the hungry with good things
and sent the rich away empty.

He has come to the aid of his servant Israel,
to remember his promise of mercy,

The promise made to our ancestors,
to Abraham and his children for ever.

LUKE 1:46-55

SESSION ONE:
PRAYING THROUGH LIFE

pilgrim

In this session we look at the importance of prayer, particularly daily prayer as foundational for the Christian life.

Opening Prayers

My soul proclaims the greatness of the Lord,
    my spirit rejoices in God my Savior;
he has looked with favor on his lowly servant.

From this day all generations will call me blessed;
the Almighty has done great things for me
    and holy is his name.

He has mercy on those who fear him,
from generation to generation.

He has shown strength with his arm
and has scattered the proud in their conceit,

Casting down the mighty from their thrones
and lifting up the lowly.

He has filled the hungry with good things
and sent the rich away empty.

He has come to the aid of his servant Israel,
to remember his promise of mercy,

The promise made to our ancestors,
to Abraham and his children for ever.

LUKE 1:46-55

**Glory to the Father and to the Son
and to the Holy Spirit;
as it was in the beginning is now
and shall be for ever. Amen.**

Loving God,
shine the light of your gospel
in and through my life each day;
help me to live as a disciple of Christ,
an ambassador for peace,
and a sign of your loving presence in the world.
Amen.

Conversation

Of the different names that the Bible gives to describe following Jesus—follower, disciple, apostle, Christian—which one makes most sense to you? What ingredients make up a good Christian life?

Reflecting on Scripture

Reading

I waited patiently for the LORD; he inclined to me and heard my cry.
²He drew me up from the desolate pit, out of the miry bog, and set my feet upon a rock,
making my steps secure.
³He put a new song in my mouth, a song of praise to our God.
Many will see and fear, and put their trust in the LORD.
⁴Happy are those who make the LORD their trust, who do not turn to the proud, to those who go astray after false gods.
⁵You have multiplied, O LORD my God, your wondrous deeds and your thoughts towards us;
none can compare with you. Were I to proclaim and tell of them, they would be more than can be counted.
⁶Sacrifice and offering you do not desire, but you have given me an open ear. Burnt offering and sin offering you have not required.
⁷Then I said, "Here I am; in the scroll of the book it is written of me.
⁸I delight to do your will, O my God; your law is within my heart."

PSALM 40:1-8

Explanatory note

The word "happy" used in this passage is translated sometimes as "blessed." Blessed has a much richer meaning than just "happy" and suggests that our joy will come from being blessed by God.

"Sacrifice" refers to the primary form of Old Testament worship, which involved bringing animals to the Temple to offer to God. Burnt offerings (or holocausts) and sin offerings were different aspects of this kind of worship. Even then, however, people recognized that sacrifice was not entirely what God wanted—delighting in God's word was far more important.

- Read the passage through once.
- Keep a few moments' silence.
- Read the passage a second time with different voices.
- Invite everyone to say aloud a word or phrase that strikes them.
- Read the passage a third time.
- Share together what this word or phrase might mean and what questions it raises.

Reflection STEPHEN COTTRELL

A Monday morning faith

What the Church does on Monday morning is just as important as what the Church does on Sunday morning. On Sunday morning it is obvious we are the Church. We are gathered together to worship God and to enjoy community together. A disciplined commitment to this aspect of our Christian life is vital. We should not leave it to chance or whim.

But on Monday morning we are still the Church. Now we are dispersed to our homes, our neighborhoods, our places of work and leisure. It is here that we are called to be the presence of Jesus, ministering in and for his world today. The Church isn't the building we gather in. The Church is the people of God. The Bible even says we are the body of Christ, each with a part to play in God's ministry and mission. Therefore we also need some sort of disciplined commitment to what it means to live as a Christian in today's world. This will affect our family life and all our relationships. It will affect our priorities and how we use our available resources of time, talents, and money. It will change

The Church isn't the building we gather in.

and shape our attitude to work and leisure, and also to the big issues of justice and peace that affect our world. You can't be a Christian for part of your life. Christian faith cannot exist in a compartment. It is either about the whole of life or it is not really about life at all.

To be sure, it takes a lifetime to allow God to so reveal God's presence within us that the whole of our life is lived to God's praise and glory and for the building of the kingdom. But by happy coincidence, a lifetime is precisely what each of us has been given. The aim of the Christian life is to live this lifetime as a member of God's Church—that is, the community of men and women centered around Jesus and being his presence in the world—and living and witnessing for the values and aspirations of God's kingdom as we have been shown them by Jesus, particularly in his teaching on the kingdom in the Beatitudes that is explored in another *Pilgrim* module.

> ### In short
> What we do on Monday morning is as important as what we do on Sunday morning. How we live as Christians affects the whole of our lives.

For discussion

- How does your church on Sunday help and equip you for your Christian life on Monday? What more could be done?
- What have you found the hardest part of living the Christian life Monday to Friday?

Discipline and desire

At the heart of this living out of the Christian vocation each day is prayer. There are many different ways of praying, and this is also explored in another *Pilgrim* module, but prayer is essential and foundational for every aspect of the Christian life. Just as a flower opens its petals to the sun on a new day, so the Christian opens herself to God in prayer. Just as the flower receives energy from the sun's heat, so the Christian is sustained and nourished by God.

We therefore need to pray each day. Just as we would not last long if we stopped eating, so the Christian life cannot be sustained for long without praying. When we pray we are in communion with God. And the art of joyful, Christian living is to find that way of praying that is right for us—which may change as we change and develop—and then weave the disciplines of prayer into daily life. For some this will mean time set aside for prayer. For others, rather than carving out a special time, the rhythms and routines of an existing daily schedule will present natural opportunities of prayer.

> *We need to pray each day.*

So pray as you walk the dog, wait on the platform for the train, or as you take your morning shower. For some, prayer will be silent and watchful. For others, it will be conversational. For others, it will be prayers from the Book of Common Prayer or books of well-loved prayers. It should always be rooted in the meditation of Scripture, and we hope the way we have reflected on the Bible at the beginning of each *Pilgrim* session will have already helped you to pray this way. And if you are absolutely stuck and don't know where to start, say grace before meals. This simple thanksgiving for God's provision will begin to weave prayer into daily life.

But all this does need discipline. There will be times when we have a great desire for God and a great desire for prayer. But there will also be dark and barren times when God feels absent. It is the discipline of daily prayer that will sustain us through a lifetime of Christian living. Like the psalmist, we will be able to sing God's praises even in the midst of trouble. This putting together of a discipline about our spiritual life and other aspects of our Christian vocation is sometimes called a rule of life. In this module we are encouraged to think what this might look like for us.

In short

Living out our daily lives as Christians involves setting aside time to spend in God's presence through prayer.

For discussion

- What ways of praying work best for you?

- How has your prayer changed and developed as you have taken part in the *Pilgrim* course?

- What elements do you think should be included in a rule of life, and how would a daily discipline about some of these things help you in your Christian vocation?

Journeying On

During this next week, think about your daily pattern of prayer and Bible reading. Make a note of when you pray and what works for you. Try out different things. Be ready to report back next time.

Concluding Prayers

Jesus, Lord of time,
hold us in your eternity.
Jesus, image of God,
travel with us the life of faith.
Jesus, friend of sinners,
heal the brokenness of our world.
Jesus, Lord of tomorrow,
draw us into your future.

**God of our pilgrimage,
you have led us to the living water:
refresh and sustain us
as we go forward on our journey,
in the name of Jesus Christ our Lord. Amen.**

Wisdom for the Journey

Loud people end up shouting noisily at God.

CYPRIAN OF CARTHAGE (C. 200–258)

It was not enough for God to make his Son our guide to the way;
he made him the way itself that we might travel with him as leader,
and by him as the way.

AUGUSTINE (354–430)

All things appear yellow to someone suffering from jaundice. Rash
judgement is a spiritual jaundice which makes everything appear
evil.

FRANCIS DE SALES (1567–1622)

I have come to know and understand more and more the profound
this-worldliness of Christianity. It is only by living completely
in this world that one learns to have faith. You must completely
abandon any attempt to make something of yourself and instead
throw yourself completely into the arms of God.

DIETRICH BONHOEFFER (1906–45)

Jesus's parables make it clear that life in the kingdom is the normal
life that is open to humanity where men and women are found in
Jesus's true relation to God—the Abba-relationship.

JOHN V. TAYLOR (1914–2001)

Detachment from things does not mean setting up a contradiction
between "things" and "God" as if God were another "thing" and
as if his creatures were his rivals. We do not detach ourselves from
things in order to attach ourselves to God, but rather we become
detached *from ourselves* in order to see and use all things in and for
God.

THOMAS MERTON (1915–68)

There are many things that can only be seen through eyes that have
cried.

ÓSCAR ROMERO (1917–1980)

SESSION TWO:
AT HOME AND AT WORK

pilgrim

In this session we begin to look at how we live out our faith every day and at the importance of Sabbath.

Opening Prayers

My soul proclaims the greatness of the Lord,
   my spirit rejoices in God my Savior;
he has looked with favor on his lowly servant.

From this day all generations will call me blessed;
the Almighty has done great things for me
   and holy is his name.

He has mercy on those who fear him,
from generation to generation.

He has shown strength with his arm
and has scattered the proud in their conceit,

Casting down the mighty from their thrones
and lifting up the lowly.

He has filled the hungry with good things
and sent the rich away empty.

He has come to the aid of his servant Israel,
to remember his promise of mercy,

The promise made to our ancestors,
to Abraham and his children for ever.

LUKE 1:46-55

**Glory to the Father and to the Son
and to the Holy Spirit;
as it was in the beginning is now
and shall be for ever. Amen.**

Loving God,
shine the light of your gospel
in and through my life each day;
help me to live as a disciple of Christ,
an ambassador for peace,
and a sign of your loving presence in the world.
Amen.

Conversation

Share with each other your experience of trying different ways of praying and of how you are developing a daily pattern of prayer.

Reflecting on Scripture

Reading

Observe the sabbath day and keep it holy, as the LORD your God commanded you. ¹³For six days you shall labor and do all your work. ¹⁴But the seventh day is a sabbath to the LORD your God; you shall not do any work—you, or your son or your daughter, or your male or female slave, or your ox or your donkey, or any of your livestock, or the resident alien in your towns, so that your male and female slave may rest as well as you. ¹⁵Remember that you were a slave in the land of Egypt, and the LORD your God brought you out from there with a mighty hand and an outstretched arm; therefore the LORD your God commanded you to keep the sabbath day.

DEUTERONOMY 5:12-15

Explanatory note

The Sabbath is the day in the Old Testament that was set aside for rest and for worship of God. For Jews, it ran from Friday evening to Saturday evening. Its name "Sabbath" means literally "rest."

A resident alien, though sounding very odd, refers simply to those who live in your town who do not come from there.

- Read the passage through once.
- Keep a few moments' silence.
- Read the passage a second time with different voices.
- Invite everyone to say aloud a word or phrase that strikes them.
- Read the passage a third time.

● Share together what this word or phrase might mean and what questions it raises.

Reflection PAULA GOODER

Freedom to rest

For many people, "Sabbath" is an alien idea. It feels like a throwback to ancient Jewish culture that has very little relevance for modern life. In fact it is as important today as it ever was.

The word "Sabbath" means simply "rest," and is a principle that is woven throughout the Bible. The two main reasons given for why God's people should rest on the Sabbath are because God rested when the creation of the world had been completed (Genesis 2:2-3) and so that the people could remember that God had freed them from slavery (Deuteronomy 5:15). Freedom is a vital strand of the Sabbath principle—only those who are free can have the luxury of a time to rest. Taking time to rest reminded God's people that it was God who had given them that freedom.

As a result, within Judaism the Sabbath is seen as a time of great joy and spiritual enrichment. Indeed Sabbaths were not just applied to people. They were also applied, among other things, to farming land. Fields were to be left "fallow" one year in every seven, so that the soil could rest and the nutrients could return. Just like people, soil needed time to rest, recuperate, and become fruitful again.

> The Sabbath is for our benefit.

In the New Testament, Jesus continued to observe the Sabbath but not to be bound by it rigidly. As he said in Mark 2:27, "The sabbath was made for humankind, and not humankind for the sabbath." In other words, the Sabbath is for our benefit, not our restriction.

For much of Christian history it was very easy to keep the "Sabbath day." Stores and restaurants would be closed and all forms of amusement removed for a day of enforced rest and worship of God. Hardly surprisingly there are few people today who would support such draconian practices, not least because they seem to have lost sight of Jesus' own teaching about Sabbath being for our benefit. But it does beg the question of how we should "observe the Sabbath day and keep it holy."

It is hard these days even to identify a single "Sabbath" day. Many people simply do not have the luxury of the same day off every week to spend with others. So we face a challenge, but it is an important challenge for each one of us to reflect on. How should we keep proper rest time? Time that reflects the recognition that we all need time to rest, recuperate, and become fruitful again. Time that lives out in practice the principle that rest is for our benefit not our restriction. Time that draws us back again to remembrance of the God who created the world in the first place and then rested.

> **In short**
> The idea of "Sabbath" is that we should have time for rest, recuperation, and rejuvenation.

For discussion

- How do you relax and recuperate? Do you have a day off a week?

- What was good and what was bad about having a strict Sunday rest time imposed on everyone?

- How do you think we might rediscover the joy of Sabbath that we find in Judaism?

The value of rest

Having a clear "Sunday" rest day implied that all rest and all worship of God took place on one day in the week. The phrase "Sunday best" still lurks in our English language. Although today very few people would wear their dressiest clothes on a Sunday, wearing your Sunday best was very important for a long time. We may not wear Sunday best clothes any more, but many of us worship God on a Sunday, and that is our "Sunday best."

This is important and right. Worshiping God with the very best that we have is a good instinct, but if we are not careful we can slip into the trap of believing that we only worship God on one day a week. Somewhat shockingly, in the book of Amos God explodes: "I hate, I despise your festivals and I take no delight in solemn assemblies" (5:21). As the passage goes on it becomes clear that God hates the festivals because the people assumed that was all they needed to do. They went to the temple, worshiped God, and then went back to abusing the poor and acting unjustly in the rest of their life.

Christianity is not a one-day-a-week religion.

Now, as then, God requires the whole of our lives to reflect worship, prayer, justice, and righteousness, Monday to Saturday as well as on Sunday. Christianity is not a one-day-a-week religion; it is a faith that should flow outwards in everything we say and do—at work and at home, with colleagues and with friends and family. God calls each one of us to live lives that reflect our faith every hour of every day—and not just to have a "Sunday best" faith.

> **In short**
>
> Although worship of God on a particular day of the week is important, that is not all God asks of us. God also calls us to live out our life of worship and faith every day of the week.

For discussion

- If you were to live an "everyday" faith, not just a "Sunday best" faith, is there anything about your life that you might need to do differently?

- Revisit the question of how the faith you celebrate on Sunday overflows into the rest of the week: what are the particular challenges of the Christian faith for your workplace? for your home?

Journeying On

During this next week, think about the balance between your worship, your rest, and your work. What takes priority? What priorities need to be shifted? Are there compromises or conflicts between one bit of your life and another? Keep a note of this and be ready to share some of your conclusions next time.

Concluding Prayers

Jesus, Lord of time,
hold us in your eternity.
Jesus, image of God,
travel with us the life of faith.
Jesus, friend of sinners,
heal the brokenness of our world.
Jesus, Lord of tomorrow,
draw us into your future.

God of our pilgrimage,
you have led us to the living water:
refresh and sustain us
as we go forward on our journey,
in the name of Jesus Christ our Lord. Amen.

Wisdom for the Journey

God has created me to do him some definite service; he has committed some work to me which he has not committed to another. I have my mission—I may never know it in this life, but I shall be told it in the next… I am a link in a chain, a bond of connection between persons. He has not created me for naught. I shall do good. I shall do his work.

JOHN HENRY NEWMAN (1801–90)

Christ must be in every home, if it is to be in any way a home of peace and love. God's plans are better than our own, and he has ordained that the training-place for his human creatures should be the home; the training-place for parents as well as children. Our task is to restore true family life for it is God's own institution, and therefore a divine thing. The home is God's institution as truly as is the church: let that be the truth that we proclaim.

MARY SUMNER (1848–1921)

The path of discipleship is narrow, and it is easy to miss one's way and stray from the path, even after years of discipleship. To confess and testify to the truth as it is in Jesus, and at the same time to love the enemies of that truth, and to love them with the infinite love of Jesus Christ, is indeed a narrow way. To believe the promise of Jesus that his followers shall possess the earth, and at the same time to face our enemies unarmed and defenseless, preferring to incur injustice rather than to do wrong ourselves, is indeed a narrow way. But if we behold Jesus Christ going on before step by step, we shall not go astray. But if we worry about the dangers that beset us, if we gaze at the road instead of at him who goes before, we are already straying from the path. For he is himself the way, the narrow way, and the strait gate. He, and he alone, is our journey's end.

DIETRICH BONHOEFFER (1906–45)

LIVING GENEROUSLY

pilgrim

In this session we look at what it means to reflect the generosity of God in our own lives.

Opening Prayers

My soul proclaims the greatness of the Lord,
　my spirit rejoices in God my Savior;
he has looked with favor on his lowly servant.

From this day all generations will call me blessed;
the Almighty has done great things for me
　and holy is his name.

He has mercy on those who fear him,
from generation to generation.

He has shown strength with his arm
and has scattered the proud in their conceit,

Casting down the mighty from their thrones
and lifting up the lowly.

He has filled the hungry with good things
and sent the rich away empty.

He has come to the aid of his servant Israel,
to remember his promise of mercy,

The promise made to our ancestors,
to Abraham and his children for ever.

LUKE 1:46-55

**Glory to the Father and to the Son
and to the Holy Spirit;
as it was in the beginning is now
and shall be for ever. Amen.**

Loving God,
shine the light of your gospel
in and through my life each day;
help me to live as a disciple of Christ,
an ambassador for peace,
and a sign of your loving presence in the world.
Amen.

How did you get on with thinking about issues of balance in your life and how the things we celebrate in worship overflow into and shape the rest of our lives, especially at work, where sometimes the things we have to do are in conflict with the values of our faith? What do you think it means to love generously?

Reflecting on Scripture

Reading

We want you to know, brothers and sisters, about the grace of God that has been granted to the churches of Macedonia; ²for during a severe ordeal of affliction, their abundant joy and their extreme poverty have overflowed in a wealth of generosity on their part. ³For, as I can testify, they voluntarily gave according to their means, and even beyond their means, ⁴begging us earnestly for the privilege of sharing in this ministry to the saints—⁵and this, not merely as we expected; they gave themselves first to the Lord and, by the will of God, to us, ⁶so that we might urge Titus that, as he had already made a beginning, so he should also complete this generous undertaking among you. ⁷Now as you excel in everything—in faith, in speech, in knowledge, in utmost eagerness, and in our love for you—so we want you to excel also in this generous undertaking.

⁸I do not say this as a command, but I am testing the genuineness of your love against the earnestness of others. ⁹For you know the generous act of our Lord Jesus Christ, that though he was rich, yet for your sakes he became poor, so that by his poverty you might become rich. ¹⁰And in this matter I am giving my advice: it is appropriate for you who began last year not only to do something but even to desire to do something—¹¹now finish doing it, so that your eagerness may be matched by completing it according to your means. ¹²For if the eagerness is there, the gift

is acceptable according to what one has—not according to what one does not have. [13]I do not mean that there should be relief for others and pressure on you, but it is a question of a fair balance between [14]your present abundance and their need, so that their abundance may be for your need, in order that there may be a fair balance. [15]As it is written,

"The one who had much did not have too much,
and the one who had little did not have too little."

2 CORINTHIANS 8:1-15

Explanatory note

"The churches of Macedonia" refers to Christian communities in northern Greece, and would have included communities in Philippi and Thessalonica among others. This letter is addressed to the Corinthian community, which was located in southern Greece. The reference in verse 15 is to Exodus 16:18.

- Read the passage through once.
- Keep a few moments' silence.
- Read the passage a second time with different voices.
- Invite everyone to say aloud a word or phrase that strikes them.
- Read the passage a third time.
- Share together what this word or phrase might mean and what questions it raises.

Reflection   JOHN PRESTON

Abundant giving

Even if a church had more money than it knew what to do with, it would still need to teach church members about giving. For as we learn to give, we find our place in God's amazing plan of generosity, and we begin to reflect God's character as we learn to live generously.

Generosity is right at the heart of God's character. God's provision is always rich—we are not given just one butterfly in creation, but over 15,000 species of butterfly. All that we have, and all that we are, are part of God's abundant giving.

> Generosity is right at the heart of God's character.

But the simple truth is that our churches do need our giving of time, skills, and money in order to fulfill the ministry and mission that God is calling us to. Indeed, that invitation to us to participate, unworthy as we are, is itself part of God's generosity.

Living generously requires us to give of all that we have—of time, hospitality, gifts, and money. The Macedonian Christians that Paul writes about in the reading we have looked at in this session knew what it was to live generously, even though they were themselves very poor and facing difficult times. Their priority was to put God first, and as they did so, they gave generously to the needs of the apostles with them, and to the collection for the church in Jerusalem.

There are many opportunities for us to give, and many ways to do so. Whether we give time, money, hospitality, or whether we give ourselves in prayer and compassion, Christian generosity is a rich tapestry of giving. This is beautifully illustrated by Jesus' parable of the Good Samaritan (Luke 10:25-37)—who gave time to stop, gave of himself by putting himself at risk in a dangerous situation, gave of his comfort in putting the injured man on his donkey and walking with him, and finally gave of his money when he got to an inn and paid for whatever care the man needed.

And here's the amazing thing—as we allow God's grace to flow through us, and give to those in need, so we find ourselves giving back to God. Matthew records Jesus teaching: "For I was hungry and you gave me food, I was thirsty and you gave me something to drink, I was a stranger and you welcomed me. I was naked and you gave me clothing" (Matthew 25:35-36).

We are called to be "Good Samaritans" as we respond generously to the situations that we encounter. But we're also called to give in a planned and regular way. While this particularly applies to money, it is also good to give our time in a regular way through finding those opportunities where we can be of service to others in church and community, perhaps as a volunteer.

> **In short**
>
> Giving is important because it allows us to find our own place in God's amazing plan of generosity. Even if the Church didn't need our money, we would need to give.

For discussion

● If we reflect on the times when we give of our time, money, and hospitality, when do we find it easiest to give? When do we find it hardest to give? Why do we think that is?

First fruits

Giving the "first fruits" has always been an important biblical principle, a radical challenge to giving ourselves first to God and only then thinking of ourselves, rather than meeting our own needs first and seeing what's left over at the end.

Christians are called to give generously. However, since what constitutes true generosity will be different from person to person, it is helpful to have some yardsticks. Here are four alternative options, as different people find different measures helpful:

1 When I set my giving in the context of my income, the percentage I'm giving away is a realistic amount. Whether or not we choose to tithe, proportionate giving is a clear step towards the challenge that those who have more are called to give more.

2 When I see that my giving in all its forms has an impact on my lifestyle, I can identify an element of sacrifice to my giving.

3 When my giving is a priority from what I receive each week or each month, rather than what's left over. Do we give as a priority or do we give from the extra? Many make their charitable contributions at the beginning of the month to indicate that they are the "first fruits."

4 When if what I give away was given back to me, it would make a real difference to me. This final yardstick personalizes our giving—what does it mean to me?

And in summary, let me bring this together with a simple thought: generous giving is vital if your church is to live out the mission that God has called it to. But generous living, in all its aspects—time, money, hospitality, and so on—is even more essential for you to become the person God has created you to be, reflecting God's image and grace.

> **In short**
>
> We are called to give the very best that we have to God, not just the scraps that are left over when we have finished doing something else.

For discussion

- Paul records the Macedonians giving "first to the Lord." If we are honest, do we give first to the Lord or only after we've taken care of our own needs? What would it look like if we gave "first to the Lord"?

- One distinctive feature of Christian giving is that what is asked of us relates to what we are given (see 1 Corinthians 8:12). So what would living generously look like for you?

Journeying On

During this next week, reflect more deeply on how you spend your money. Be aware that it reveals your priorities. Also think and pray about how you use your time and gifts. Is it marked by generosity?

Concluding Prayers

Jesus, Lord of time,
hold us in your eternity.
Jesus, image of God,
travel with us the life of faith.
Jesus, friend of sinners,
heal the brokenness of our world.
Jesus, Lord of tomorrow,
draw us into your future.

God of our pilgrimage,
you have led us to the living water:
refresh and sustain us
as we go forward on our journey,
in the name of Jesus Christ our Lord. Amen.

Wisdom for the Journey

Do not have Jesus Christ on your lips, and the world in your heart.

IGNATIUS OF ANTIOCH (*C.* 35–*C.* 107)

Never despise homeless people who are stretched out on the ground as if they merit no respect. Ask who they are and discover their worth.

GREGORY OF NYSSA (*C.* 330–94)

In my view there is nothing so frigid as a Christian who does not care about the salvation of others. It is useless to plead poverty in this respect, for the poor widow who put two copper coins in the treasury will be your accuser.

JOHN CHRYSOSTOM (C. 347–407)

Those who wish to make a place for the Lord should rejoice not in private success but in the common good. Let us, therefore, abstain from the love of private property or even from the possession of it altogether. Instead, let us make a place for the Lord.

AUGUSTINE OF HIPPO (354–430)

We must serve God with the gifts he has given us.

BENEDICT (480–550)

Hold the things of this world in such a way that you are not held by them. Earthly goods must be possessed: do not let them possess you. The things that you own must be under the control of your mind. Otherwise, if your mind is dominated by the love of earthly things, you will become possessed by your own possessions. Let temporal possessions be what we use, eternal things what we desire. Let temporal goods be for use on the way, eternal goods be desired for when we arrive at our journey's end.

GREGORY THE GREAT (540–604)

Choose rather to want less, than to have more.

THOMAS À KEMPIS (C. 1380–1471)

In all the affairs and duties of life, we should be sure to look more to God than we do at them. When our duties demand our undivided attention, we should still be sure that from time to time we cast a look towards God, rather like sailors who in setting their course for port look more at the stars of heaven than the open sea. In so doing God will work with you and in you and for you, and you will not labor in vain but will be filled with God's consolation.

FRANCIS DE SALES (1567–1622)

You can give without loving. But you cannot love without giving.

AMY CARMICHAEL (1867–1951)

I do not believe one can settle how much we ought to give. I am afraid the only safe rule is to give more than we can spare. In other words, if our expenditure on comforts, luxuries, amusements, etc., is up to the standard common among those with the same income as our own, we are probably giving away too little. If our charities do not at all pinch or hamper us, I should say they are too small. There ought to be things we should like to do and cannot do because our charitable expenditures excludes them.

C. S. LEWIS (1898–1963)

Remember this—you can't serve God and Money, but you can serve God with money.

SELWYN HUGHES (1928–2006)

No one has ever become poor by giving.

ANNE FRANK (1929–45)

SESSION FOUR:
IN ALL MY RELATIONSHIPS

pilgrim

In this session we look at how faith in the God who is Father, Son, and Holy Spirit shapes and changes all our relationships.

Opening Prayers

My soul proclaims the greatness of the Lord,
    my spirit rejoices in God my Savior;
he has looked with favor on his lowly servant.

From this day all generations will call me blessed;
the Almighty has done great things for me
    and holy is his name.

He has mercy on those who fear him,
from generation to generation.

He has shown strength with his arm
and has scattered the proud in their conceit,

Casting down the mighty from their thrones
and lifting up the lowly.

He has filled the hungry with good things
and sent the rich away empty.

He has come to the aid of his servant Israel,
to remember his promise of mercy,

The promise made to our ancestors,
to Abraham and his children for ever.

LUKE 1:46–55

**Glory to the Father and to the Son
and to the Holy Spirit;
as it was in the beginning is now
and shall be for ever. Amen.**

Loving God,
shine the light of your gospel
in and through my life each day;
help me to live as a disciple of Christ,
an ambassador for peace,
and a sign of your loving presence in the world.
Amen.

Conversation

What conclusions did you come to about your own giving and generosity? Not just your money but also your time and gifts? How does "living generously" in response to the God who has given us everything in Christ begin to change our relationship with others, especially those closest to us, but also those we find most difficult or different?

Reflecting on Scripture

Reading

Just then a lawyer stood up to test Jesus. "Teacher," he said, "what must I do to inherit eternal life?" [26]He said to him, "What is written in the law? What do you read there?" [27]He answered, "You shall love the Lord your God with all your heart, and with all your soul, and with all your strength, and with all your mind; and your neighbor as yourself." [28]And he said to him, "You have given the right answer; do this, and you will live."

[29]But wanting to justify himself, he asked Jesus, "And who is my neighbor?" [30]Jesus replied, "A man was going down from Jerusalem to Jericho, and fell into the hands of robbers, who stripped him, beat him, and went away, leaving him half dead. [31]Now by chance a priest was going down that road; and when he saw him, he passed by on the other side. [32]So likewise a Levite, when he came to the place and saw him, passed by on the other side. [33]But a Samaritan while travelling came near him; and when he saw him, he was moved with pity. [34]He went to him and bandaged his wounds, having poured oil and wine on them. Then he put him on his own animal, brought him to an inn, and took care of him. [35]The next day he took out two denarii, gave them to the innkeeper, and said, 'Take care of him; and when I come back, I will repay you whatever more you spend.' [36]Which of these three, do you think, was a neighbor to the man who fell into the hands of

the robbers?" [37]He said, "The one who showed him mercy." Jesus said to him, "Go and do likewise."

LUKE 10:25-37

Explanatory note

"A lawyer" at the time of Jesus would have been someone who was an expert in the Jewish law, so this lawyer would probably have been a scribe, a Levite, a Priest, or a Pharisee (i.e. quite possibly someone mentioned in the story!).

The Levite and the Priest may have feared that the man was dead. If they had touched him they would not have been allowed to serve in the temple.

Samaria, which lies between Judea and Galilee, was inhabited by people whose religious roots were the same as those of the Jews but who had developed their faith differently. There are still Samaritans living in Israel and Palestine, but in 2015 they numbered fewer than 800.

- Read the passage through once.
- Keep a few moments' silence.
- Read the passage a second time with different voices.
- Invite everyone to say aloud a word or phrase that strikes them.
- Read the passage a third time.
- Share together what this word or phrase might mean and what questions it raises.

Reflection   RACHEL TREWEEK

Transforming relationships

> *Relationship is at the heart of who God is.*

Relationship is at the heart of who God is: Father, Son, and Holy Spirit. The Bible tells a story of a people made in God's image and made to live in relationship with God, in relationship with neighbor, and in relationship with self. The ideal of this relationship is reflected in the creation narratives at the beginning, but it is not long after that we see their first fracturing (Genesis 1–3).

But God is in the business of making all things new. The Bible's closing pages present a picture of creation redeemed and God's kingdom fully revealed (Revelation 21:1-5). God's people are restored to perfect relationship with each other and with their God. This is made possible through Christ's death and resurrection, and as God goes on bringing into being that which does not exist (Romans 4:17), Christ's followers are called to reflect the breaking through of God's kingdom in every relationship. This is rarely easy and always risky. That was true of the Samaritan with a stranger; and it is just as true in our relationships of deep intimacy or encounters with colleagues or friends.

Our pride and deep fear of humiliation and failure can drive us to relate in ways that are neither life-giving for ourselves nor for others. The Samaritan *might* have acted from a selfish motive, such as a need to be needed or to be seen as a hero; or perhaps he was driven by a desire to be special or always to succeed. Yet this story is told by Jesus to illustrate what it means to be a good *neighbor*, and therefore the Samaritan is clearly someone who truly desired the well-being of another. This was costly not only financially but also in terms of time, emotion, and risk (a point that would not have been lost on Jesus' Jewish audience, who looked down on Samaritans and had virtually no social contact with them). Here is someone of difference choosing to act in the interest of the other. This is about having the mind of Christ (Philippians 2:1-8).

> **In short**
>
> As Christians we are called to make risky relationships with those who are different from us, in the same way as the Samaritan did in Luke 10.

For discussion

- What does it mean to you to be "made for relationship"? How have your relationships with others made you and shaped who you are?

- And how has your growing relationship with God changed you and shaped you, especially in your daily life and in your other relationships?

Serving others and living with difference

As we grow in personal relationship with Christ and experience the ongoing work of the Holy Spirit in our lives, we are called to live relationships that enable mutual flourishing and transformation. And it must be true for all our relationships. Whether it is between close and intimate friends, marriage partners, parents and children, or colleagues at work, each relationship is a place of encounter that offers the potential for joy and pain to be shared, for love and trust to grow, for support and for faithful commitment and nurture to be given and received. In this each person in the relationship has the potential to grow more like Christ and become more the person God created them to be. And the deeper the relationship, such as that between a married couple, the greater the commitment and the greater the potential for growth in Christlike self-giving and receiving.

Each relationship is a place of encounter.

This generous love is best revealed to us in Christ's total self-giving on the cross. But vulnerability, commitment, and faithfulness are qualities asked of us in every relationship. And there is always the danger that fear and selfishness mean we end up risking nothing, giving nothing away, and rejecting or dismissing others. It is this we must guard against. The Samaritan allowed his heart to be moved, and this led to an intentional choice to serve another. Seeking the well-being of others is not about being driven by "should" and "ought" and is never to be confused with degradation of self or the permitting of abuse.

When Christ takes on the role of a slave and washes the feet of his disciples (John 13:1-15), we read that: "Jesus, knowing...that he had come from God and was going to God, got up from the table" (v. 3). Jesus knew who he was. My love of neighbor will be impoverished if I do not: commit to continually discovering who *I am* in a place of both repentance and hope; dare to hear God's "yes"; accept God's love and grace in abundance; and grow in understanding of self (1 John 3:1). It is only from this place that I can truly serve others.

Serving others also requires living with difference. We are created in God's image as unique individuals. The concept of being the body of Christ is one that affirms diversity (1 Corinthians 12:12-14), and yet so often when we encounter difference in others we experience fear and threat. In a world that struggles with difference and the conflict that often emerges, Christ's followers have rich treasure to offer when they demonstrate what it means to "disagree well."

If the Samaritan and the injured man had encountered each other in the future, they would have still been men with profound differences. However, I like to think that there would have been a bond between them that meant they exhibited respect, trust, love, and grace as they remained committed to relationship in a place of difference.

In short
Vulnerability, commitment, and faithfulness are qualities asked of us in every relationship.

For discussion

- In what ways do you take Christlike risk in your relationships?
- What needs to change in order for your relationships to reflect more distinctively the love of Christ?
- How might we love one another better in places of difference?

Journeying On

During this next week, reflect more deeply on your *closest* human relationships and your *trickiest* human relationships. How are they places where Christ can be known and revealed and where you can grow in Christlike giving and service?

Concluding Prayers

Jesus, Lord of time,
hold us in your eternity.
Jesus, image of God,
travel with us the life of faith.
Jesus, friend of sinners,
heal the brokenness of our world.
Jesus, Lord of tomorrow,
draw us into your future.

God of our pilgrimage,
you have led us to the living water:
refresh and sustain us
as we go forward on our journey,
in the name of Jesus Christ our Lord. Amen.

Wisdom for the Journey

In Christian teaching there can be no double-standards. Whatever is unlawful for a woman is equally unlawful for a man. Men and women were redeemed together for one price, and together have been called into the assembly of the Christian church. With what arrogance or with what sort of conscience do men think they can do with impunity things which are unlawful for men and women equally?

CAESARIUS OF ARLES (*C.* 470–543)

There are four qualities which must be tested in a friend: loyalty, right intention, discretion and patience, so that you can entrust yourself to them securely.

AELRED OF RIEVAULX (1109–67)

If there be anywhere on earth [where] a lover of God is always kept safe from falling, I know nothing of it, for it was not shown me. But this was shown: that in falling and rising again we are always kept in the same precious love.

JULIAN OF NORWICH (1342–1416)

One form of gentleness that we should all practice is towards ourselves. We should never get irritable with ourselves, fretting at our imperfections. It is entirely reasonable to be displeased and feel sorry when we have done something wrong, but we should refrain from being full of self-recrimination, fretful, or spiteful to ourselves.

FRANCIS DE SALES (1567–1622)

There is no need for peculiar conditions in order to grow in the spiritual life, for the pressure of God's Spirit is present everywhere and at all times. Our environment itself—our home and our job—is the medium through which we experience His moulding action and His besetting love… And this quality of quietness, ordinariness, simplicity, with which the saving action of God enters history, endures from the beginning to the end.

EVELYN UNDERHILL (1875–1941)

To love another as a person we have to love them for what they are in themselves, and not for what they are to us. We have to love them for their own good, not for the good we get out of them. And this is impossible unless we are capable of a love which "transforms" us, so to speak, into the other person, making us able to see things as they see them, to love what they love, to experience the deeper realities of their own life as if they were our own. Without sacrifice, such transformation is utterly impossible.

THOMAS MERTON (1915–68)

Community life is not something extraordinary or heroic, reserved only for an elite of spiritual heroes. It is for us all; it is for every family and every group of friends committed to each other. It is the most human way of living; and the way that brings the greatest fulfillment and joy to people. As people live in communion with the Father, they enter more and more into communion with one another; they open their hearts to the smallest and the weakest. Being in communion with the smallest and the weakest, their hearts are touched and the waters of compassion flow forth; in this way they enter more deeply into communion with the Father.

JEAN VANIER (1928–)

Love at first sight is easy to understand; it's when two people have been looking at each other for a lifetime that it becomes a miracle.

AMY BLOOM (1953–)

pilgrim

In this session we look at how the Christian life requires us to be involved in the affairs of the world and to witness to God's kingdom of peace and justice every day.

Opening Prayers

My soul proclaims the greatness of the Lord,
    my spirit rejoices in God my Savior;
he has looked with favor on his lowly servant.

From this day all generations will call me blessed;
the Almighty has done great things for me
    and holy is his name.

He has mercy on those who fear him,
from generation to generation.

He has shown strength with his arm
and has scattered the proud in their conceit,

Casting down the mighty from their thrones
and lifting up the lowly.

He has filled the hungry with good things
and sent the rich away empty.

He has come to the aid of his servant Israel,
to remember his promise of mercy,

The promise made to our ancestors,
to Abraham and his children for ever.

LUKE 1:46-55

**Glory to the Father and to the Son
and to the Holy Spirit;
as it was in the beginning is now
and shall be for ever. Amen.**

Loving God,
shine the light of your gospel
in and through my life each day;
help me to live as a disciple of Christ,
an ambassador for peace,
and a sign of your loving presence in the world.
Amen.

Conversation

In the last session we thought about how faith in Christ transforms relationships, and even started to think about one of Jesus' most difficult injunctions: to love our enemies. Share with each other how you have been thinking about your own relationships, the challenging ones as much as any other. How might this generous self-giving to all affect and challenge some of the deep-seated injustices that we see around us in the world?

Reflecting on Scripture

Reading

Show us your steadfast love, O LORD, and grant us your salvation. [8]Let me hear what God the LORD will speak, for he will speak peace to his people, to his faithful, to those who turn to him in their hearts. [9]Surely his salvation is at hand for those who fear him, that his glory may dwell in our land.

[10]Steadfast love and faithfulness will meet; righteousness and peace will kiss each other.

[11]Faithfulness will spring up from the ground, and righteousness will look down from the sky.

[12]The LORD will give what is good, and our land will yield its increase.

[13]Righteousness will go before him, and will make a path for his steps.

PSALM 85:7-13

- Read the passage through once.
- Keep a few moments' silence.
- Read the passage a second time with different voices.
- Invite everyone to say aloud a word or phrase that strikes them.
- Read the passage a third time.
- Share together what this word or phrase might mean and what questions it raises.

Venturesome love

It's not fair!

Such protests are familiar. We care passionately about fairness, but God isn't about fairness: God treats us better than we deserve. God is deeply generous. How else are we to make sense of Jesus telling the story of the workers in the vineyard? In this story from Matthew 20, Jesus illustrates the nature of the kingdom of God: the generous landowner gives a day's pay to both those who labored all day and those who worked for only a few hours. Such generosity prompted those who worked all day to protest that it's not fair. It is not guaranteed that the generosity that characterizes God's kingdom will be well received.

God is deeply generous.

God's unfailing love, to use the words of the psalmist, propels us to live generously and challenge the injustices that insult God's kingdom. However, efforts to confront injustice, just like the generous owner of the vineyard, will be said to be naïve or wasteful (echoes here of the woman who lavishes expensive perfume on Jesus).

Following Jesus by standing up for those who face injustice is uncomfortable terrain. Dom Hélder Câmara, winner of a Nobel Peace Prize for his work with the poor in Brazil, expressed this tension aptly: "When I give food to the poor they call me a saint. When I ask why the poor have no food they call me a Communist."

Confronting injustice requires willingness to embrace *struggle*, and this is an important aspect of Christian maturity. The free embrace of a struggle often singles us out because for many their aim in life may be just the opposite: they may be aiming to avoid struggle and extra hassle—unless it serves self-interest. Discipleship implies the willing embrace of struggle because following Jesus involves venturesome love. Discipleship is not to be mistaken for doing jobs in church—it is far more adventurous terrain than this.

For discussion

- How might you be called to a discipleship going beyond "helping in the church" to "seeking God's kingdom for the world"?

- Share experiences of when you have been involved in confronting injustice. What did it feel like? What opposition did you meet? How did it change your faith and your prayers?

Embracing commitment

Confronting the injustices of our world may also break our heart. Solidarity with those who face injustice is unlikely to increase our confidence in our good works. Rather, it will bring deeper awareness of our personal sins and our complicity in sinful systems. Those who are alongside homeless people, asylum seekers, or displaced thousands in refugee camps often record how they have been brought to a deeper awareness of their own sin and the inadequacy of their efforts. Following the way of Jesus and willingly embracing a struggle for peace and justice will deepen our recognition of the sin of the world as well as our own sin. When confronting the injustice of the world, we come to know ever more clearly our need for a savior.

Confronting injustice is one of the major challenges for Christians—it is unlikely to make us popular, it means we have to turn idleness into commitment and it may break our heart; and there is further hazard, because, let's be frank, so often it

We have to turn idleness into commitment.

is hard to know what to do for the best. This might be in relation to people we know or communities or nations in distress, as well as in relation to a host of persistent social issues that pluck at our heart strings. Prayer matters when we are confronted by these arduous challenges. Prayer, far from inaction, strengthens us *for* action. Prayer opens the door to the Holy Spirit, and prayer can give the gift of timing enabling momentum to grow. Prayer feeds our imagination and gives us courage and hope in the struggle, and it helps to keep us honest to acknowledge that we may be as much a part of the problem as we are of the solution.

Through prayer we cry to God about injustice, and each of us will have specific injustices that rile us—perhaps the vulnerability of children in war-torn places, the distress associated with enduring mental illness, famine, abuse of women, or the brutalizing of young men. The list is long and personal. Your prayer burden is that distinct issue that angers, distresses, and frustrates you. We pray about injustice not because there is nothing that we can do but because prayer makes us ready to act. Prayer makes warriors of us. To be a warrior means to have the necessary prowess and readiness to respond when the time comes. Prayer equips us as warriors, willing and able to confront the injustices of our world.

> **In short**
> We pray about injustice because prayer makes us ready to act.

For discussion

- What is your prayer burden? What is that distinct issue of justice and compassion that makes you cry out to God because it angers, distresses, and frustrates you?

- What difference might your prayer make?

- How might God be calling you to be the answer to your own prayer?

Journeying On

In the book of Ecclesiastes it says that "in much wisdom is much vexation, and those who increase knowledge increase sorrow" (Ecclesiastes 1:18). The Beatitudes call us to lamentation—Blessed are those who mourn—and to hunger and thirst for what is right. During this week, think deeply about those issues of injustice that you have identified in this session and how your prayers and actions can be part of God's solution. What will it mean for you to be a peacemaker like this? What opposition or misunderstanding will you face? Where is God asking you to stand up and be counted?

For next week, the final session, start to think about how you would describe the distinctive Christian life we are called to live as members of God's Church and as citizens of God's kingdom. We will each be invited to share our conclusions.

Concluding Prayers

Jesus, Lord of time,
hold us in your eternity.
Jesus, image of God,
travel with us the life of faith.
Jesus, friend of sinners,
heal the brokenness of our world.
Jesus, Lord of tomorrow,
draw us into your future.

God of our pilgrimage,
you have led us to the living water:
refresh and sustain us
as we go forward on our journey,
in the name of Jesus Christ our Lord. Amen.

Wisdom for the Journey

Resolve to imitate God's justice and no one will be poor.

GREGORY OF NAZIANZUS (329–89)

Not to give to those in need what is to you superfluous is akin to fraud.

AUGUSTINE OF HIPPO (354–430)

Truth is the perfect correlation of mind and reality; and this is actualized in the Lord's person. If the gospel is true and God is, as the Bible declares, a living God, the ultimate truth is not a system of propositions grasped by a perfect intelligence, but is a personal being apprehended in the only way in which persons are ever apprehended, that is by love.

WILLIAM TEMPLE (1881–1944)

To pray is to quench our thirst at the source of love… This love unites us deeply, converts us, makes us turn away from ourselves and towards others; it inspires us to take up the struggles for a better world… Love is a lever against egoism in ourselves, in others, and in all structures of society.

MICHEL QUOIST (1921–97)

And then Easter happened. Jesus rose from the dead. The incredible, the unexpected happened. Life triumphed over death, light over darkness, love over hatred, good over evil. That is what Easter means—hope prevails over despair … Oppression and injustice and suffering can't be the end of the human story, freedom and justice, peace and reconciliation, are his will for us, black and white, in this land and throughout the world. Easter says to us that despite everything to the contrary, his will for us will prevail, love will overcome hate, justice over injustice and oppression, peace over exploitation and bitterness.

ARCHBISHOP DESMOND TUTU (1931–)

SESSION SIX:
TREADING LIGHTLY ON THE EARTH

In this session we look at our relationship with the earth itself.

Opening Prayers

My soul proclaims the greatness of the Lord,
    my spirit rejoices in God my Savior;
he has looked with favor on his lowly servant.

From this day all generations will call me blessed;
the Almighty has done great things for me
    and holy is his name.

He has mercy on those who fear him,
from generation to generation.

He has shown strength with his arm
and has scattered the proud in their conceit,

Casting down the mighty from their thrones
and lifting up the lowly.

He has filled the hungry with good things
and sent the rich away empty.

He has come to the aid of his servant Israel,
to remember his promise of mercy,

The promise made to our ancestors,
to Abraham and his children for ever.

LUKE 1:46-55

**Glory to the Father and to the Son
and to the Holy Spirit;
as it was in the beginning is now
and shall be for ever. Amen.**

Loving God,
shine the light of your gospel
in and through my life each day;
help me to live as a disciple of Christ,
an ambassador for peace,
and a sign of your loving presence in the world.
Amen.

Conversation

Share with each other your conclusions about the injustices that God is asking you to pray about and how your own actions might become the answer to your own prayers. Then begin to share your reflections on the great injustice that is our misuse and exploitation of the earth itself. What is your experience of or reaction to climate change?

Reflecting on Scripture

Reading

Then God said, "Let us make humankind in our image, according to our likeness; and let them have dominion over the fish of the sea, and over the birds of the air, and over the cattle, and over all the wild animals of the earth, and over every creeping thing that creeps upon the earth."
[27]So God created humankind in his image,
   in the image of God he created them;
   male and female he created them.
[28]God blessed them, and God said to them, "Be fruitful and multiply, and fill the earth and subdue it; and have dominion over the fish of the sea and over the birds of the air and over every living thing that moves upon the earth." [29]God said, "See, I have given you every plant yielding seed that is upon the face of all the earth, and every tree with seed in its fruit; you shall have them for food. [30]And to every beast of the earth, and to every bird of the air, and to everything that creeps on the earth, everything that has the breath of life, I have given every green plant for food." And it was so. [31]God saw everything that he had made, and indeed, it was very good. And there was evening and there was morning, the sixth day.

GENESIS 1:26-31

- Read the passage through once.
- Keep a few moments' silence.
- Read the passage a second time with different voices.
- Invite everyone to say aloud a word or phrase that strikes them.
- Read the passage a third time.
- Share together what this word or phrase might mean and what questions it raises.

Reflection   DAVID WALKER

Safeguarding the integrity of creation

The moment usually comes about 30 seconds after I've been introduced to somebody. They take in my face, my clerical collar and episcopal cross, and then their eyes drop down and linger, just slightly too long to be natural, on my feet. Then I remember. I remember that, in most of the circles in which I move, sandals with no socks is not conventional dress. It's an important moment of recollection, because it reminds me of why I sport such unusual footwear. I go, lightly shod, in order to tread lightly upon the earth.

Francis of Assisi has a lot to answer for in this matter. I discovered him first in college, and from then on he and the religious communities he founded seemed to be everywhere my journey took me. Francis trod lightly on the earth; famously he would pick up worms that had strayed onto footpaths, setting them down somewhere they would be less likely to be harmed. Grounded in his powerful attachment to the suffering Jesus on the cross he was no sentimentalist, but he saw in every aspect of creation, even those creatures and objects feared or despised, something of the glory of the Creator.

The whole created universe is God's handiwork, and you and I are inheritors of the responsibility as stewards of creation given to humanity in the very first chapter of Genesis. That responsibility is set out forcefully and succinctly in the last of the Five Marks of Mission of the worldwide Anglican Communion, of which The Episcopal Church is part: "To strive to safeguard the integrity of creation and sustain and renew the life of the earth." It's a responsibility that was brought home vividly to me at the 2008 Lambeth Conference of Anglican bishops when I found myself in conversation with a colleague whose entire diocese is likely to disappear beneath rising sea levels within a lifetime.

> *The whole created universe is God's handiwork.*

For that bishop, as for the vast consensus of the worldwide scientific community, the question is no longer whether humanity is changing the climate. It's a matter of how severe is our impact and what we can do to reduce it to sustainable levels. More acutely, can we sustain creation without condemning the world's developing nations to permanent poverty? There is, within mainstream Christianity, widespread acceptance of the importance of that fifth Mark of Mission. In recent years, during Lent, The Episcopal Church has encouraged congregations to learn about their ecological footprint—the impact each has on land, water, and energy.

In short
God's call on each one of us is to tread lightly on the earth.

For discussion

- Is our Christian responsibility under God primarily to the well-being of future humanity or to the creation itself? Does it make a difference?

- What do you see as the most urgent environmental challenge facing the world today? What is the first thing that needs to be done about it?

Renewing the face of the earth

Concern about climate change, along with wider environmental awareness, is not the exclusive property of Christians. Others, of all faiths and none, both share our concern and offer leadership in making practical responses. Dedicated environmentalists, who are not also managing commitments to other religious priorities, may outstrip us in both zeal and achievement. So what, if anything, is the distinct Christian contribution to the cause of treading lightly upon the earth?

Francis can help us again here. His passionate embrace of voluntary poverty was rooted in a profound experience of the love that held Christ to the cross. Born the son of a rich merchant, he discovered that our true worth is not measured in possessions but in the value that God places on us. He no longer needed to measure himself against his fellow citizens by the weight of his purse or the opulence of his parties. Indeed he found that material goods all too readily became an idolatrous distraction. While only a great saint may travel quite that far, we can take from him a distinctively Christian sense of sufficiency and adequacy in what we own and what we use up. A more modest environmental footprint suffices because our exploitation of the world's resources has ceased to be a constituent of our self-worth.

From the Christian tradition comes the notion of prophetic action. A few low-wattage electric bulbs may not of themselves prevent global warming, but they are not lights hidden under a bushel. Whenever we take some action that acknowledges God's reign, we erect signposts to the kingdom. From the 35 solar panels on the Episcopal Diocese of Vermont's property providing electricity to their school to the composting and recycling initiatives of St. Matthew's Episcopal Church in Evanston, Illinois, Christian individuals and organizations make visible statements of how to tread more lightly. What we can't do everywhere, we still do somewhere.

I am part of it all.

And in that instant, when my newest acquaintance looks just too long at my feet, I remember that I am part of it all.

For discussion

- Are there things you have deliberately done, or consciously avoided, in order to tread lightly upon the earth? Is there something you feel you ought to do but struggle to manage?

- Is the price of sustaining God's creation a lowering of your own standard of living? If so, is that price too high?

Journeying On

How would you describe what it means to live a distinctive Christian life? Share your thoughts in turn, and then think about how you will go on developing a life of prayer and generosity that will affect and shape all that you do, from your carbon footprint, to your use of time and money, to your most intimate relationships. It might be helpful to write this down. This can then be the basis for a rule of life that, though reviewed and amended often, can last a lifetime.

Concluding Prayer

Jesus, Lord of time,
hold us in your eternity.
Jesus, image of God,
travel with us the life of faith.
Jesus, friend of sinners,
heal the brokenness of our world.
Jesus, Lord of tomorrow,
draw us into your future.

God of our pilgrimage,
you have led us to the living water:
refresh and sustain us
as we go forward on our journey,
in the name of Jesus Christ our Lord. Amen.

Wisdom for the Journey

God has given abundantly to all the basic needs of life, not as a private possession, not restricted by law, not divided by boundaries, but as common to all, amply and in rich measure. His gifts are not deficient in any way because he wants to give equality of blessing to equality of worth, and to show the abundance of his generosity.

GREGORY OF NAZIANZUS (329–89)

If I knew I was to die tomorrow, I would plant a tree today.

MARTIN LUTHER (1483–1546)

Christ has no body now on earth but yours,
no hands but yours,
no feet but yours.
Yours are the eyes through which to look out at
Christ's compassion to the world.
Yours are the feet with which he is to go about
doing good.
Yours are the hands with which he is to bless men now.

TERESA OF ÁVILA (1515–82)

You never enjoy the world aright till the sea itself floweth in your veins, till you are clothed with the heavens, and crowned with the stars, and perceive yourself to be the sole heir of the whole world, and more than so, because men are in it who are every one sole heirs as well as you. Till you can sing and rejoice and delight in God, as misers do in gold, and kings in sceptres, you never enjoy the world.

THOMAS TRAHERNE (C. 1636–74)

The world is charged with the grandeur of God.
It will flame out, like shining from shook foil;
It gathers to a greatness, like the ooze of oil
Crushed. Why do men then now not reck his rod?
Generations have trod, have trod, have trod;
And all is seared with trade; bleared, smeared with toil;
And wears man's smudge and shares man's smell: the soil
Is bare now, nor can foot feel, being shod.
And for all this, nature is never spent;
There lives the dearest freshness deep down things;
And though the last lights off the black West went
Oh, morning, at the brown brink eastward, springs—
Because the Holy Ghost over the bent
World broods with warm breast and with ah! bright wings.

GERARD MANLEY HOPKINS (1844–89)

If we do not at least try to manifest something of Creative Charity in our dealings with life, whether by action, thought, or prayer, and do it at our own cost—if we roll up the talent of love in the nice white napkin of piety and put it safely out of the way, sorry that the world is so hungry and thirsty, so sick and so fettered, and leave it at that: then, even that little talent may be taken from us. We may discover at the crucial moment that we are spiritually bankrupt.

EVELYN UNDERHILL (1875–1941)

We believe this is God's world and we need to walk lightly and humbly within and upon it. We are stewards of that which comes from and returns to God. We believe that all of life is precious and indeed that God has so designed creation that for one part to flourish all must flourish. Further, we believe that God has created the world in balance: land and water, light and darkness, evening and morning, sowing and reaping, winter and summer, birth and death, belong together; to exploit one to the detriment of another is to put all in jeopardy.

LAMBETH CONFERENCE 2008

NOTES

Opening Prayers for all sessions
Common Worship, Daily Prayer, London, Church House Publishing, 2005, p. 607 and Lucien

Concluding Prayers for all sessions
Common Worship, Times and Seasons, London, Church House Publishing, 2006, p. 233 and *New Patterns for Worship*, London, Church House Publishing, 2002, p. 291.

Session One
Cyprian of Carthage (c. 200–58), *On the Lord's Prayer*, 4.

Augustine of Hippo (354–430), *Commentary on Psalm* 109 (Heb. Ps. 110), 3.

Francis de Sales (1567–1622), *Introduction to the Devout Life*, iii, 28.

Dietrich Bonhoeffer (1906–45), *Letters and Papers from Prison*, ed. Eberhard Bethge, 2nd edn, London, SCM, 1971, p. 369.

John V. Taylor (1914–2001), *The Go-Between God*, SCM Press, London, 1973, p. 135.

Thomas Merton (1915–68), *Seeds of Contemplation*, New York, Burns & Oates, 1961; London, 1962, 1977, 1999. © Thomas Merton, Continuum Publishing, used by permission of Bloomsbury Publishing Plc.

Óscar Romero (1917–1980), *Sermon.*

Session Two
John Henry Newman (1801–90), *Meditations and Devotions*, ed. Ian Ker, London, Darton, Longman & Todd, 2010 (first published 1893), p. 11.

Mary Sumner (1848–1921), Address to the Mothers' Union in Winchester.

Dietrich Bonhoeffer (1906–45), *The Cost of Discipleship*, 1937; trans. R. H. Fuller, SCM, London, 1959, p. 170.

Session Three
Ignatius of Antioch (c. 35–c. 107), *Letter to the Romans*, 1.

Gregory of Nyssa (c. 330–394), *Homily* 1 "*On the Love of the Poor.*"

John Chrysostom (c. 347–407), *Homily* 20 "*On the Acts of the Apostles.*"

Augustine of Hippo (354–430), based on his exposition of Psalm 132.

Benedict of Nursia (480–550), *Rule*, Prologue.

Gregory the Great (540–604), *Homily* 36 "*On the Gospels,*" ii.

Thomas à Kempis (c. 1380–1471), *Imitation of Christ.*

Francis de Sales (1567–1622), *Introduction to the Devout Life*, 111, 10.

Amy Carmichael (1867–1951), Missionary to India.

C. S. Lewis (1898–1963), *Mere Christianity*, New York, Macmillan, 1952, p. 86.

Selwyn Hughes (1928–2006).

Anne Frank (1929–45), *Diary of Anne Frank*, 1952.

Session Four
Caesarius of Arles (c. 470–543), *Sermon* 43, 3.

Aelred of Rievaulx (1109–67), *On Spiritual Friendship*, III, 61.

Julian of Norwich (1342–1416), *The Revelations of Divine Love.*

Francis de Sales (1567–1622), *Introduction to the Devout Life*, III, 9.

Evelyn Underhill (1875–1941), *Mysticism.*

Thomas Merton (1915–68), *The Power and Meaning of Love*, Burns & Oates, London, 1976, p. 8. © Thomas Merton, Continuum Publishing, used by permission of Bloomsbury Publishing Plc.

Jean Vanier (1928–), *Community and Growth*, London, Darton, Longman & Todd, rev. edn, 1989, p. 94.

Amy Bloom, (1953–).

Session Five
Gregory of Nazianzus (329–89), *Oration* 14 "*On the Love of the Poor,*" 23.

Augustine of Hippo (354–430).

William Temple (1881–1944), *Readings in St John's Gospel*, London, Macmillan, 1939.

Michel Quoist (1921–97), *Living Words*, Dublin, Gill & Macmillan, 1978, p. 38.

Archbishop Desmond Tutu (1931–), *Crying in the Wilderness*, Grand Rapids, MI, Eerdmans, 1982, p. 83.

Session Six
Gregory of Nazianzus (329–89), *Oration* 14 "*On the Love of the poor,*" 25.

Martin Luther (1483–1546), source unknown.

Teresa of Ávila (1515–82).

Thomas Traherne (c. 1636–74), *Centuries of Meditations*, 1, 19.

Gerard Manley Hopkins (1844–89), "God's Grandeur"

Evelyn Underhill (1875–1941), *Mysticism.*

"Statement on Safeguarding the Integrity of Creation," Lambeth Conference 2008.